In Your Time

Finding Your Unique Path Through Grief and Healing:
A 45 Day Companion for Healing

In Your Time

Finding Your Unique Path Through Grief and Healing:
A 45 Day Companion for Healing

VICTORIA CELESTE
Endy Writes Publishing

Acknowledgment is made for the use of work developed by Elisabeth Kübler-Ross, a renowned psychologist who pioneered the concept of the five stages of grief. This framework has provided a valuable understanding of the myriad emotions that individuals may experience following a loss. Reference: Kübler-Ross, E. (1969). On Death and Dying. Macmillan.

Acknowledgment is made for the use of Bible verses from the New King James Version (NKJV). These verses have provided valuable insights and spiritual guidance throughout the book. Reference: New King James Version. Nashville: Thomas Nelson.

Library of Congress Control Number: 2023910380
ISBN-13: 978-0-9797138-4-2
Endy Writes Publishing
Florida
Printed in the United States of America

Dedication

In Your Time is devoted wholeheartedly to my dear mother, Linda B Bell. Her legacy continues to illuminate our lives, even in her absence. Her life, guidance, genuine love, and thoughtful gifts have etched an indelible mark on the world. Her influence has made me the person I am today.

Reminiscing on my college days, I recall studying the human lifespan with an emphasis on death, dying, and the intricate stages of grief. During my mother's final transition, I witnessed her move through these same stages. After weeks of quiet withdrawal, she summoned us to her hospital bed one early morning, articulating clearly and firmly about our respective roles. This moment echoed my academic lessons about the stages of death, exposing a profound truth about the ephemeral nature of life.

Our lives were invaded by cancer when mom was diagnosed with the disease. A woman of unyielding strength, she had previously vanquished ovarian and thyroid cancers. Despite quitting smoking twelve years earlier, she found herself waging war against another form of cancer- lung cancer, one brought on by a misdiagnosed backache. I vividly remember her last days in the hospital, her last meal on Christmas, and ultimately succumbing to her illness the subsequent month.

When God inspired me to write this book, to be released around Mother's Day, I questioned, "Why me?" The response was, "Why not you?" I've tasted the bitter pill of grief and various losses, more than most could conceive.

My first encounter with grief was in middle school when Nigel, a young man I tutored tragically lost his life in a car accident. His entire family— his mother and siblings—all perished in the incident. The pain was palpable, even though I could not fully comprehend its depth at my tender age. However, it's not solely the loss of loved ones that creates a void. The grief of past life seasons, transitional phases, and evolving relationships can stir intense pain within us. Reflecting on my journey, I recognize that these experiences have shaped me into the person I stand as today.

My journey through grief has been a lesson in embracing, rather than denying or dismissing, the harsh reality of loss. I've learned to live through it, recognizing that grief is an intensely personal process with no universally 'right' way to traverse it.

There were moments when I teetered on the brink of collapse under the crushing weight of my grief. Balanced on the precipice of despair, feeling the overwhelming burden of my grief threatening to crush me. Yet, in those moments, God ceaselessly whispered to me, "You've rediscovered the art of living." This profound truth echoes in the hearts of all those who have tasted loss.

We possess the power to heal, the strength to reconstruct our lives, and indeed, the resilience to not just survive, but to wholeheartedly thrive and live once more.

Introduction

Welcome to this deeply personal devotional, where we embark on a journey that touches the very core of our being—grief. It's a journey we all must take at some point in our lives, a journey that challenges us in unimaginable ways. As a life coach, I have witnessed firsthand the transformative power that grief holds, how it can shape us, and how it can lead to profound personal growth and a rekindled relationship with faith.

Within the pages of this devotional, you will discover more than just a book. It is a companion, a spiritual counselor, and a guide, blending together personal reflections, shared experiences, and practical wisdom. This journey of healing doesn't follow a one-size-fits-all blueprint. It demands self-compassion, a willingness to seek support, and, above all, patience. Healing takes time, and it is important to honor your own unique process.

Embrace the freedom to skip a specific area if it does not resonate with you in this season of life. You may find that certain devotions speak to you more deeply than others. Allow yourself the freedom to explore and reflect on the topics that resonate with your soul, for it is in these moments of connection that profound transformation can occur. Trust your instincts and follow the path that feels right for you.

Whether you find yourself at the beginning of your grief journey or navigating the treacherous terrain of loss, this book aims to be a constant companion. It offers actionable guidance, comforting messages, and reminders of God's boundless love and mercy. In times of sorrow and confusion, it serves as a beacon of hope, reminding you that there is light even in the darkest of moments.

Grief, in all its rawness, forces us to confront our deepest emotions. Yet, within that vulnerability lies an opportunity for growth and a strengthening of our connection with God and those around us. As you embark on this transformative voyage, you will learn how to harness the pain of loss and turn it into a catalyst for personal growth, deepening your faith, and fortifying your spirit.

Always remember, you are never alone in this journey of grief. There is a divine presence, an unwavering comforter, who walks with you through the valleys and the mountains, holding your hand and guiding you towards hope and healing.

In obedience to a divine call, I humbly share this deeply personal testament—a journey through grief and a testament to the indomitable resilience of the human spirit. I share my lessons, struggles, and hopes with the sincere wish that they may bring you solace, guidance, and the strength to persevere. But remember, do it at your own pace. There is no rush. Healing happens in your time, and may this devotional serve as a steadfast companion on your path.

Stages Of Grief

These stages are not set in stone. They might not occur sequentially, you might revisit stages, or even skip stages entirely. Some stages may feel more intense than others, and the duration of each stage varies widely.

Remember, grief is not a one-size-fits-all experience. It's as unique as the individual experiencing it. Embrace your emotions, let yourself grieve in your own way, at your own pace. Don't hesitate to seek help from loved ones or professionals if the burden feels too heavy. This journey is yours, but you needn't walk it alone.

Psychologist Elisabeth Kubler-Ross pioneered the concept of the five stages of grief, a framework many find useful to understand the whirlwind of emotions they might experience after a loss.

1. Denial: Here, we often grapple with the sheer weight of the loss, our minds struggling to comprehend the magnitude of it. Shock and disbelief can create a buffer against the raw pain.

2. Anger: As the walls of denial crumble, we may find anger rushing in. Frustration and resentment might get directed towards others, towards the world, or even towards the person we've lost.

3. Bargaining: This stage can involve a lot of 'what ifs' and 'if only.' We might find ourselves yearning to strike a deal with a higher power, seeking a way to reverse our devastating loss.

4. Depression: A sense of profound sadness, hopelessness, and disinterest in once-loved activities can characterize this stage, as the reality of the loss sinks in.

5. Acceptance: This isn't about feeling "okay" with the loss. Instead, it's about acknowledging the loss, seeing a future beyond it, and gradually re-engaging with life, albeit in a changed way.

Divinely Commissioned

Answering The Call, Touching Hearts, And Unleashing Divine Healing Power

Sitting on the beach, with the gentle waves lapping against the shore, I find solace and inspiration as I pour my heart into this sacred task that God has entrusted me with.

Writing this book is both a healing blessing and a weighty mandate. It's an honor to be chosen as a vessel to share with you, to offer a glimmer of hope to those who may be traversing the treacherous terrain of grief. But with this privilege comes a sense of responsibility, a deep longing to ensure that my words resonate with authenticity and touch countless lives in profound ways.

As I reflect on the unique journey of grief, I'm reminded that it is a path walked by each individual in their own way and time. There is no one-size-fits-all approach to healing. Grief is as personal as a fingerprint, as individual as the footprints left in the sand. Each person carries their own pain, their own memories, and their own way of finding solace. In this book, I aim to shatter the clichés, to offer a raw and transparent account of some my own experiences, in the hopes that it may serve as a guiding light for others. It is my sincerest desire that these pages become a source of comfort, understanding, and encouragement for those who have felt the weight of loss.

The task before me is great, but I draw strength from knowing that I am not alone in this endeavor. The words flow through me, guided by God and I trust that they will find their way into the hearts and lives of those who need them most. With every stroke of the pen, I pray that this book becomes a vessel of healing, a source of divine intervention, and a catalyst for transformation.

This journey of writing is more than just words on a page; it is a divine calling, a precious work entrusted to me by God. As I sit on this beach, feeling the weight of this mandate, I am humbled and awestruck by the opportunity to touch countless lives. God's presence is with me, guiding my words and infusing them with healing power.

May this work be a lighthouse in the storm, a beacon of light for all who seek solace in the midst of grief.

Day 1: Desperate for Tears

Finding Strength in Unshed Tears

In the depths of my grief, I found myself yearning for the cathartic release of tears. I longed to let the floodgates open and allow my sorrow to pour out, but the tears remained stubbornly unshed. It felt as though my body had betrayed me, trapping me in a limbo of pain and confusion. The weight of this unexpressed grief threatened to shatter the fragile peace I had managed to find, leaving me feeling disconnected from the world.

As the days turned into weeks, I grappled with the notion that my inability to cry somehow made my grief less valid. The guilt and shame that accompanied my emotional paralysis only served to deepen my sense of isolation. I wasn't sure if it was my way of being strong for everyone else or if one day my heart would physically break. But in the quiet moments of introspection, I began to understand that my journey through grief was a personal one, and that the absence of tears did not diminish the intensity of my pain. I came to realize that there are countless ways to express grief, and that each person's experience is unique.

In time, I found solace in connecting with others who had faced similar struggles and discovered new ways to express my grief. Through their support and understanding, I learned that it's not the tears that define our grief, but the love we hold for those we've lost.

Romans 8:26 - "In the same way, the Spirit helps us in our weakness. We do not know what we ought to pray for, but the Spirit himself intercedes for us through wordless groans"

Day 2: Uniquely Yours

Your Journey Through Grief

It's okay to slow down, to take a breath, to reflect upon the journey you have taken so far.

Just like a traveler wandering through unknown territories, you might come across unexpected detours or roadblocks. Sometimes, you might even feel like you're walking in circles, returning again and again to the same spot of sorrow. But remember, every journey, including yours, is filled with such moments. They do not signify failure; rather, they are part of the path towards healing.

Your journey is a testament to the love you've shared, love that continues to thrive even in the face of loss. This love is your compass, guiding you through the labyrinth of grief. It's the torch that lights your path, even on the darkest nights.

As you carry on with your journey, remember that it's okay to seek help when you need it. Reach out to loved ones, lean on those who offer support, and know that professional help is available, too. Grief can be a solitary path at times, but you don't have to walk it alone. The love and support that surround you are like signposts on your journey, reminding you that you are cherished and not alone.

In this journey of grief, there's no predetermined timeline, no map with a clearly marked route. The journey is yours, to take at your own pace, in your own time. But no matter how daunting the road may appear, remember, you possess an inner strength, a resilience forged from love and sorrow. As you navigate your way through the terrain of grief, trust in this strength. Trust in the love that continues to guide you. And trust in the promise of healing and renewal that lies ahead.

Proverbs 16:9 - "In their hearts humans plan their course, but the LORD establishes their steps."

Day 3: The Day the Tears Finally Flowed

The Closet's Cry: "Grief Unleashed"

The day the tears finally flowed was a moment I'll never forget. I remember it like it was yesterday. It was four years after my mom died, and I was in a new loving relationship. I was sitting in the closet when it happened – I lost it. The scream was so loud that my then-boyfriend, now husband of 17 years, ran into the room and asked what was wrong. Without knowing the cause, he just held me and said, "Whatever it is, we will get through it."

As the tears cascaded down my cheeks, I experienced a profound sense of relief and release. It felt as if the dam within me had finally burst, releasing the torrent of emotions I had been holding back for so long. It was as though the weight of my unexpressed grief had finally begun to lift, allowing me to breathe a little easier and see the world with clearer eyes.

With each tear that fell, I felt a growing sense of connection to my mom, as if the act of crying was a bridge that connected our hearts across the chasm of loss. The outpouring of emotion served as a reminder that I was not alone in my grief, and that the love we shared transcended the boundaries of life and death. That was the day that I felt safe enough, I guess, to let go, knowing that if I totally lost it, I had someone there who would help me pick up the pieces.

As I continue to navigate the unpredictable journey of grief, I carry with me the memory of the day the tears finally flowed, a turning point in my healing process. I have learned to embrace the moments of sorrow, understanding that they are an essential part of my journey towards acceptance and peace. Through the tears, I honor the memory of my mom and loved ones, cherishing the love that we shared, and finding the strength to carry that love forward into the world.

Matthew 5:4 - "Blessed are those who mourn, for they will be comforted.

Day 4: Boundaries of the Heart

Shielding Your Grief Journey from Unwanted Voices

It's an oddity of pain - especially the kind steeped in the profound loss - that it frequently morphs into a public spectacle for those on the periphery of your world. The unsolicited advice pours in, overwhelming and constant, the attempts to relate, even the sheer audacity of others trying to dictate how you should feel or heal - it can feel as though your personal grief is being swallowed up, eclipsed by the noise of everyone else's opinions. Navigating your own complex emotional landscape is challenging enough, without the added stress of filtering through the barrage of well-intentioned, but all too often, misguided attempts at consolation from those who have never ventured into the bleak terrain of your shoes.

Allow me to assert this unequivocal truth - your grief is entirely your own. It is as distinctive and individual as the relationship you cherished with the one you've lost. No one else, no matter their intentions, can truly grasp the profound depths of your sorrow or the intricacies of your journey to healing. It's entirely acceptable to feel frustrated by the seemingly insensitive comments or misguided advice. It's within your right to request space, to demand understanding rather than advice, to call for a listening ear rather than a speaking mouth.

Remember, true empathy lies in aligning with people right where they are - not where we might wish them to be. Your journey through grief is a solo expedition, and no one else can navigate it for you. Take solace in the understanding that your emotions are valid, your process is uniquely yours, and it's entirely okay to request others to respect that. In a world that often scrambles to provide quick solutions, sometimes the most potent healing force we can offer is to simply listen, truly hear, and steadfastly hold space for the other person's pain.

Your heart's symphony is a composition of its own, echoing with the strains of loss, yet resilient in its hope for a brighter melody. Let this be your guiding principle: Your grief journey, while traversed alone, does not have to be a path of isolation. Draw strength from the shared human experiences, understanding that each of us is uniquely equipped to handle our trials. Amid the cacophony of well-meaning but often dissonant advice, tune into your own rhythm, your own healing frequency, and let it guide you towards tranquility and self-understanding.

Remember, in this symphony of life, your solo is as important as any other, and it deserves to be heard with empathy and respect.

Romans 12:15 "Rejoice with those who rejoice, weep with those who weep."

Day 5: Love, Betrayal and the Road to Forgiveness

Navigating Dual Grief and The Power of Letting Go

Grief, in its rawest form, holds a mirror to life's most profound truths and unmasked vulnerabilities. It was a double-edged sword when my mother, my beacon of strength and love, was on her deathbed and the revelation of betrayal from a loved one came crashing down on us. My aunt, one of my mother's best friends and sister-in-law, had manipulated her trust to forge her name on an insurance policy, seeking selfish gains at such a solemn time. At times, I wanted to pray for her, times I wanted to lay hands on her, and there were moments I wanted her to feel the pain and betrayal my mom felt. It felt as if I was navigating through a storm, where I was not just grieving the impending loss of my mother, but also the death of a relationship that I once held dear.

Loss, in its myriad forms, can hit us in ways we least expect. It's an uncanny journey where the familiar contours of relationships can suddenly morph into unfamiliar landscapes, leaving us grappling with feelings of hurt, anger, and a sense of profound loss. As I navigated this duality of grieving my mother and the relationship with my aunt, I realized the complex emotions were intertwined. The hurt wasn't just mine but was my mother's too - a pain that she carried in the last days of her life. The reality was bitter, yet I knew it had to be faced.

The road to forgiveness is seldom easy, particularly when the pain feels insurmountable. It's a choice we make, often against the heavy tide of resentment and anger. But it is a necessary one. To forgive my aunt was to honor the love and strength of my mother. It was to say, "I acknowledge the pain, but I choose not to let it define me or our memories." It was to give myself permission to grieve and yet to heal. To forgive is to make peace with the past, and to courageously face the future. It's to affirm that even amidst hurt, I can reclaim my power, my peace. In forgiving my aunt, I wasn't condoning her actions, but liberating myself from the shackles of anger and resentment.

As I continue this journey of healing, I carry in my heart the invaluable lessons of love, trust, betrayal, forgiveness, and, most importantly, the enduring strength and spirit of my mother.

Matthew 6:14-15 - "For if you forgive men their trespasses, your heavenly Father will also forgive you. But if you do not forgive men their trespasses, neither will your Father forgive your trespasses."

Day 6: The Finality of It All

Navigating Grief after Losing Both Parents: Honoring Their Legacy, Finding Strength in The Journey

The profound and life-altering experience of losing a parent takes an even deeper toll when both parents depart. It can feel as if the very ground you're standing on has crumbled away, leaving you without the foundation you've relied on for so long. Navigating the world without their loving guidance and unwavering presence can seem daunting, and the grief you experience is unique and deeply personal. You mourn not only the loss of individuals who brought you into this world, but also your connection to your roots and the legacy they've left behind.

Remember, though, that the love you shared with your parents transcends life and death. Their spirits live on within you, forever shaping your heart and soul. You find comfort in the memories you've made, the lessons they taught you, and the values they instilled. Through the love they poured into you, you become the torchbearer of their legacy.

Grieving the loss of both parents is a complex journey, filled with profound sadness and the responsibility to honor their memory. It leads you on a path of self-discovery, where you navigate the depths of your emotions and learn to redefine your identity without their physical presence. Faith becomes your stronghold, providing you with the strength to believe that your parents are now in a peaceful place, watching over you with love and guiding you through the storm.

This sacred journey of grief, remembrance, and self-discovery is not one you undertake alone. Your parents' love continues to shape you, reminding you of who you are and what you are capable of. As you delve into the depths of sorrow, find solace in the eternal bond you share and draw strength from the memories, values, and love they've imparted.

Remember, you're not alone. Your parents' love continues to guide you, and as you navigate grief, you'll discover an inner strength, resilience, and a deeper appreciation for the enduring power of love.

Psalm 30:5: "Weeping may endure for a night, but joy comes in the morning." Hold on to the promise of a new dawn, filled with healing, hope, and peace.

Day 7: Confronting the Final Goodbye

Learning to Live with Permanent Loss

There's an undeniable finality in death that can shake us to our core. The thought of 'never' can seem incomprehensible – never hearing their laughter again, never feeling their touch, never sharing another moment. The permanence of this loss can be an overwhelming reality to confront, a bitter pill that we are forced to swallow. In these moments, we find ourselves grappling with the inescapable truth that life, as we knew it, has changed irrevocably.

Yet, even amid this profound pain, there's a need for acceptance. Not an acceptance that minimizes our grief, but an acceptance that allows us to begin to understand our loss. It's about acknowledging the absence, the void that's been left, and learning how to navigate the new reality of our lives without them.

This isn't about 'moving on' in the traditional sense, but rather moving forward, carrying our grief with us, and learning to live with it. It's a journey that requires patience and self-compassion, as we each grieve and heal in our own unique ways and time.

Though we may never see our loved ones again in this life, we can find solace in our faith, comfort in our memories, and strength in our love that transcends the confines of this physical world. Your journey through grief is your own, and in your time, you will find your way. They may be gone from your sight, but they will forever remain in your heart.

2 Corinthians 1:3-4 provide comfort and hope in this journey: "Blessed be the God and Father of our Lord Jesus Christ, the Father of mercies and God of all comfort, who comforts us in all our affliction, so that we may be able to comfort those who are in any affliction, with the comfort with which we ourselves are comforted by God."

Day 8: Grieving the old me

The Path of Self-Rediscovery After Loss

The words that once echoed the depths of my grief now serve as testament to the journey. As you read this, know that the rhythm of your life, though it may now reverberate with the cacophony of loss, can find its own peaceful harmony. When you face the mirror, you might see a reflection molded by sorrow, but remember, it doesn't have to be haunted by it. It can reflect a person who, just like me, is capable of navigating the storm of grief and emerging changed yet resilient. Battles you wage today between the memory of your former self and the reality of your current existence can settle into acceptance. Yearning for the comfort of a lighter, unburdened heart can transform into a newfound appreciation for the strength and resilience that arise from trials.

The chapters of your past, which may now be marked by pain and transformation, will not solely define you. Instead, they can help you appreciate the growth, victories, and even losses that sculpt your present. The journey towards self-love and acceptance, though fraught with struggle, can reveal in you a resilience and strength that wouldn't exist without adversity. Indeed, storms change us, but they can also unfold a version of ourselves that is stronger and more resilient than ever before.

In the crucible of grief, you can find transformation, rising from the ashes of your former self. The pain you endure can shape you, sculpt you into an individual you couldn't foresee becoming. This is a journey of acceptance, learning to embrace the new you while acknowledging the loss of what was. While you might not be exactly where you envision yourself to be, you're far removed from where you used to be. The battles you fight, the scars you carry, and the growth you achieve are badges of honor, symbolizing the transformation you're undergoing.

In this transformation lies the strength to conquer and the power to rise above. Through it all, remember that the past is a place of reference, not residence, and you too can stand tall, proud of your journey and the resilience it has instilled within you. You are not alone, and every step you take, however small, is a victory in your journey of healing and growth. Never lose hope, for you are stronger than you know.

Isaiah 43:18-19 - "Do not remember the former things, nor consider the things of old. Behold, I will do a new thing, now it shall spring forth; shall you not know it? I will even make a road in the wilderness and rivers in the desert."

Day 9: Where Love Lingers

Through The Looking Glass of Grief Reflections in Places Once Shared

In the vast tapestry of grief, there are threads that weave through the fabric of our lives, connecting us to the places we once frequented with the person we have lost. The mere thought of visiting these familiar spots can stir a mix of emotions—anticipation, longing, and a profound sense of loss. The restaurants where you shared laughter and meals, the trips that became cherished memories, the favorite parks where you found solace, the hotels that provided a temporary haven, and the stores where you embarked on countless adventures—all hold a piece of your heart. Amid grief, these places become sacred ground, carrying the weight of nostalgia and the sting of absence.

As you walk the path of grief, know that your experience of visiting these places is deeply personal. Embrace the flood of emotions that wash over you, for they are a testament to the love and connection you shared. The grief and surrealness that accompanies these visits may be overwhelming at times but remember that healing is not a linear process. Allow yourself the space to remember, to mourn, and to find solace in these familiar surroundings. Each visit becomes an opportunity for reflection, growth, and honoring the beautiful moments you shared with your loved one.

Amidst the bittersweet memories, find strength in the knowledge that you are not alone on this journey. Seek out companions who can offer a listening ear, a compassionate heart, and a guiding light. Share your stories, reminisce about the laughter and joy, and lean on them for support. They will become your anchors, providing comfort and understanding as you navigate the complexities of grief. Together, you can uncover the healing power within these familiar places, transforming them from reminders of loss to symbols of resilience and the enduring power of love.

Though the grief and surrealness of revisiting these cherished locations may evoke waves of sorrow, there is a positive twist awaiting you. Within the depths of your pain, there lies the opportunity for growth, resilience, and the discovery of new meaning. As you honor the memories and navigate the complexity of emotions, you will uncover the strength to create new chapters in your life. These places that once held treasured memories can become the backdrop for new experiences, where you forge new connections, find solace, and weave the threads of your own healing journey. So, my dear friend, as you embark on these poignant visits, know that you carry the love and legacy of your loved one within you. Embrace the grief, embrace the surrealness, and embrace the possibilities that await you as you find healing and embrace life once more.

Psalm 34:18 - "The LORD is near to those who have a broken heart and saves such as have a contrite spirit."

Day 10: What signs did I miss?

Shifting Shadows: The Unseen Battle

In the aftermath of losing a dear friend to suicide, it's not uncommon to find ourselves fixated on the past, searching for clues we may have missed and wondering how we could have intervened. The guilt weighs heavily on our hearts, as if we were somehow responsible for not noticing the signs. But what if we shift our perspective, viewing this tragic event through a different lens, allowing ourselves to find healing and growth?

We can imagine the void left by our loved one as a space to plant seeds of change, a fertile ground for nurturing empathy and understanding for others who may be silently struggling. Instead of dwelling on the guilt, we can use our pain as a catalyst for forging connections and creating a safe space for open and honest conversations about mental health. By doing so, we not only honor the memory of our dear friend, but we also give hope to those who may be suffering in silence.

Amid sorrow, we can choose to embrace the transformative power of grief, using our experience to make a difference in the world. As we journey through the healing process, let's support one another and share our stories, actively listening to the experiences of others who have faced similar loss. Through these connections, we create a legacy of empathy, awareness, and hope, honoring the memory of our loved one and working to prevent future tragedies.

By adopting this unique perspective, we recognize that our loved one's memory lives on within us, driving us to make a positive impact on the lives of others. In this way, we can build a world where no one feels alone in their struggle and where hope and healing are always within reach. Our hearts will never forget the pain of loss, but with time and understanding, we can transform that pain into a force for change and find solace in the knowledge that our loved one's life has inspired us to create a more compassionate world.

Matthew 11:28-30: "Come to me, all you who are weary and burdened, and I will give you rest. Take my yoke upon you and learn from me, for I am gentle and humble in heart, and you will find rest for your souls. For my yoke is easy and my burden is light."

Day 11: Why God Why?

The Enigma of Faith

I've often found myself at the precipice of a paradox, staring into the void of 'why'. Why did God allow this tragedy? Why did the fabric of my world have to unravel in such a brutal, unforgiving way? Why God? It's a question that can tug at the corners of your faith, a question that I know I'm not supposed to ask.

It's a human inclination to question, to seek understanding, especially when life hands us a script we never wished to read. But with every tear shed, every sleepless night, and every silent prayer, I've come to realize that my faith isn't hinged on the answers to my 'why'. Instead, it's anchored in the undeniable truth that even amidst the storm, God is sovereign.

So, if you, like me, are grappling with the 'why', let's remember together that faith isn't a solution to the puzzle of life. Instead, it's the assurance that even when the pieces don't fit, God is still masterfully at work. His ways are higher, His thoughts are greater, and His love for us remains steadfast. Let's lean into this love, knowing that while we may not always understand the 'why', we are eternally held in the arms of the One who does.

Isaiah 55:8-9, "For my thoughts are not your thoughts, neither are your ways my ways, declares the LORD. For as the heavens are higher than the earth, so are my ways higher than your ways and my thoughts than your thoughts."

Day 12: Dreams So Real

Grieving Between the Awake and Asleep

In the dark corners of the night, when the world stands still and the walls of reality seem to blur, dreams can become a double-edged sword. There, in the realm of dreams, she is alive, vibrant as ever. These dreams, so potent in their realism, become a sanctuary, a hidden meeting place where you can once again see her, hear her, feel her. But each morning, reality presses in, and waking up feels like losing her all over again.

These dreams can be a torment, their visceral reality a cruel reminder of what was lost. But perhaps, in another light, they can also be viewed as a testament to the love you shared. The love so profound, so intense, that even the boundary of life and death cannot hold it captive. Yes, the mornings may bring with them a sense of loss that's almost unbearable, but the nights, the nights bring her back to you, if only for a fleeting moment.

Grief is challenging, and it's okay to feel lost in it. But remember, these dreams, as painful as they might be, are also a reminder of the love that still exists. With each passing night and day, you are navigating through the stormy seas of your grief, and even though it might not feel like it, you are moving forward. Hold onto the love, the memories, and let them guide you through.

Psalms 34:18- "The Lord is close to the brokenhearted and saves those who are crushed in spirit." With time, healing will come, and you will find peace, both in your dreams and when you wake."

Day 13: When is it okay to love again?

The Divine Path to Accepting Love Once More

The pain of losing a spouse is something I cannot comprehend, but I have listened to the stories of those who have courageously shared their journey with me. The profound heartache and overwhelming loneliness that follows such a loss are beyond words. Grief is a deeply personal process, and there is no timeline or right way to navigate it. One question that often arises during the healing journey is: "When is it okay to move on and open my heart to a new relationship?" It's a question that carries immense weight and requires delicate consideration.

Through the shared experiences of others, I have come to understand that the love shared with a late spouse remains an everlasting memory. It is not something to be forgotten or replaced, but rather cherished and celebrated. Those who have found the strength to embrace new love have taught me that it is not a betrayal of the past, but a testament to the resilience of the human spirit and the transformative power of love. It is a way to honor the memory of the one who is gone while also honoring the life that continues to unfold.

As you journey through your own grief, remember that healing takes time and that your heart's pace is unique to you. There is no rush to find new love or to move on from the pain. When the time feels right and your heart is ready, it is okay to seek new connections and allow love to enter your life again. Embracing love does not diminish the love you had for your late spouse; instead, it becomes a testament to your own capacity for healing and growth. It is an invitation to create new beginnings and find joy in the present, while honoring the past.

"In the midst of grief's darkness, there is a glimmer of hope that beckons us to embrace love again. Trust the wisdom of your heart and honor the pace at which it heals. When the time is right, open yourself to the possibility of new connections and allow love to restore hope and light in your life. You have the strength within you to embrace love once more, not as a replacement, but as a testament to your resilience and the infinite capacity of the human heart to heal and grow. May your journey be filled with grace, love, and the unwavering knowledge that you are deserving of a joyful and fulfilling life."

Ecclesiastes 3:1-4 1 "There is a time for everything, and a season for every activity under the heavens: 2 a time to be born and a time to die, a time to plant and a time to uproot, 3 a time to kill and a time to heal, a time to tear down and a time to build, 4 a time to weep and a time to laugh, a time to mourn and a time to dance"

Day 14: That's Our Song

Vessels of memories, how music sustains the bond beyond farewell

When I hear Stephanie Mills, MJ-Off the Wall, or a Patti LaBelle song, I think of my mama. Grief is a tapestry of memories, interwoven with the melodies that formed the soundtrack of our lives. For me, the songs of Stephanie Mills, Michael Jackson's "Off the Wall," and the soulful voice of Patti LaBelle are not just music; they are a direct line to my mama's spirit. Each time these songs fill the air, they evoke a flood of emotions and transport me back to the moments shared with her. They are the soundtrack of our bond, the melodies that carried us through both joyous and challenging times. Grief is unique to everyone, and for me, these songs have become a lifeline, a way to keep my mama's presence alive in my heart.

As I journey through the grieving process, these songs hold a power that goes beyond mere notes and lyrics. They are vessels of memories, encapsulating the love, laughter, and warmth that my mama brought into my life. When Stephanie Mills sings "Never Knew Love Like This Before," I am instantly transported to our kitchen, where we danced and sang together, filling the room with laughter. MJ's "Off the Wall" takes me back to us working out together and late-night drives with the car windows down, our voices harmonizing to the rhythm of the music. And when Patti LaBelle's voice soars, I can almost feel my mama's embrace, her unconditional love enveloping me. These songs become a bridge, connecting me to the precious moments and treasured memories I shared with her.

In the midst of grief, the power of music cannot be underestimated. It has the ability to stir emotions, evoke memories, and bring solace to our weary hearts. As I reflect on the impact, I am reminded that grief is a deeply personal journey. Each person has their own unique triggers, their own songs that carry the essence of their loved ones. It is a testament to the power of connection, that even in the depths of loss, we can find comfort and a sense of closeness through the music that resonates with our souls. So, let us embrace the songs that remind us of our loved ones, for in doing so, we keep their spirit alive, and their love continues to guide us through the ebb and flow of grief.

In the symphony of grief, music becomes the conductor of our emotions, weaving together memories, love, and healing. The songs that remind us of our loved ones are not mere background noise; they are the threads that connect us to the precious moments we shared. Embrace the power of music, for it holds the key to unlocking the floodgates of emotions and keeping the spirit of our loved ones alive. In the melodies that stir our souls, we find solace, strength, and a reminder that love transcends even the depths of grief. So, let the music play on, and let the memories guide us towards healing and a renewed sense of purpose.

Isaiah 66:13 - "As one whom his mother comforts, so I will comfort you; And you shall be comforted in Jerusalem."

Day 15: From Battlefield to Homefront-Finding a New Normal

Redefining Love, Healing, And Rebuilding Together

When my husband returned from war, I held my breath, anticipating the joyful reunion that I had dreamed about for months. But as I looked into his eyes, I knew that something had changed. The weight of the war had etched lines of pain and weariness on his face, and his eyes held a distant gaze that mirrored the horrors he had witnessed. In that moment, I realized that our journey towards a new normal would not be the fairy tale reunion I had envisioned. Grief, in its unique form, had infiltrated our lives, reshaping our relationship and altering the trajectory of our future. As a wife, I had to navigate the complexities of my own grief, while holding space for the wounded soul that returned to me.

The journey towards a new normal after war was a dance of both hope and heartache. I discovered that grief is not solely reserved for those who have lost loved ones; it can also manifest in the aftermath of trauma and upheaval. The wife's new normal is a delicate balance of honoring the pain and loss that her husband endured, while also finding the strength to redefine their relationship in light of the scars they both carry. Each day brought its own unique challenges and victories, as we learned to communicate in a language woven with compassion, patience, and understanding. It was a path filled with stumbling blocks and triumphs, where resilience and love became the foundation upon which we rebuilt our lives.

In the midst of grief's embrace, I discovered the power of resilience and the ability to adapt to our new circumstances. We may never be the same as we were before the war, but we can embrace the opportunity to create a new normal, one that honors the strength and courage that brought us through the darkest moments. It is in the depths of our grief that we uncover the limitless capacity of the human spirit to heal, to love, and to thrive amidst adversity. The wife's new normal is not a destination but an ongoing journey of growth and transformation. As we navigate this uncharted territory, let us remember that even in the face of pain and uncertainty, we have the power to redefine our lives and find beauty in the midst of brokenness.

The wife's journey towards a new normal after her husband returns from war is a testament to the resilience of the human spirit. Grief may reshape our lives, but it does not define us. In the face of unimaginable challenges, we discover our strength to adapt, to love, and to rebuild. It is through the depths of our grief that we find the wellspring of courage that propels us forward. Embrace the journey, dear wife, and know that you have the power to create a new normal that is marked by healing, growth, and a love that endures. Your story is a testament to the triumph of the human spirit, inspiring others to find their own path of resilience and restoration.

Proverbs 3:5-6 - "Trust in the Lord with all your heart and lean not on your own understanding; in all your ways submit to him, and he will make your paths straight."

Day 16: Grace in the Gaps

Granting Grace to Those Unsure of How to Support You

Grief is a language that is not easily spoken or understood. It is a silent symphony of emotions that echoes through our very being. We yearn for others to comprehend our pain, to offer comfort and support in our darkest hours. But not everyone possesses the ability to navigate this uncharted territory with ease. They may stumble, say the wrong things, or inadvertently cause more pain. Yet, it is important to remember that their intentions are often rooted in love and a genuine desire to help.

In the realm of grief, where emotions run deep and the landscape of the heart is forever altered, we embark on a journey that is uniquely our own. It is a path marked by pain, resilience, and the ever-present longing for understanding and solace. Yet, as we navigate this terrain, we often encounter a perplexing reality: those around us may struggle to know how to be there for us or find the right words to say. In these moments, it is crucial to extend grace - both to ourselves and to those who may fall short of our expectations.

During times of grief, let us surround ourselves with a diverse network of support - friends, family, spiritual counselors, and guides who can provide comfort and guidance. Seek out those who can lend an empathetic ear, offer a shoulder to lean on, or simply sit with you in silence. They may not have all the answers, but their presence and willingness to be there for you is a gift in itself. Allow their love and understanding to nourish your spirit and remind you that you are not alone on this journey.

In conclusion, dear friend, extend understanding and patience, for they too may be grappling with their own uncertainties. Embrace the power of connection and empathy, and together, we can weave a tapestry of healing and support that transcends the boundaries of grief.

1 Peter 4:8 "And above all things have fervent love for one another, for 'love will cover a multitude of sins."

Day 17: This isn't happening!

Mama...

In the blink of an eye, life can take an unexpected turn, shattering our sense of safety and normalcy. When I first heard the news that my mother had cancer, the world seemed to stop spinning. Suddenly, everything seemed to move at a lightning pace, leaving me grappling with the reality that she had tumors all over her body. A storm of emotions consumed me - fear, confusion, and yet, a glimmer of hope that she would emerge victorious in this battle.

The reality of the situation felt unbearable, like a heavy weight pressing down on my chest. I struggled to come to terms with this new reality, repeating the words, "This isn't happening" like a mantra, desperately wishing to wake up from this nightmare.

In the midst of this emotional tempest, it is essential to remember that we are not isolated in our sorrow. We are all connected through the common threads of human experience, and our grief resonates with others who have faced similar trials. During these moments, it is crucial to seek comfort from the support network of friends, family, and our faith. As we confront the complex emotions of loss, we must also embrace the courage and resilience that lie within us. Each person's journey through grief is unique, but together, we can find the strength to weather the storm.

Hope serves as a guiding light, leading us through the darkest moments of our lives, shining brightly when our path seems uncertain and obscured. While we mourn the loss of those dear to us, let us also cherish the moments and memories that they left behind. In doing so, we pay tribute to their lives and the love they bestowed upon us. As we heal, we not only honor their memory but also discover our own capacity for growth and compassion.
United, we can draw from one another's strength, and with time, emerge from the depths of sorrow to embrace life with newfound wisdom and love.

Psalm 34:18 "The Lord is close to the brokenhearted and saves those who are crushed in spirit."

Day 18: Embracing the Lessons in Loss

My baby pictures were in that storage!

The pain of loss can come in many forms, leaving us feeling broken and helpless. I remember that day in Atlanta, GA, when I received the voicemail, notifying me that I had only one hour to save our belongings from being auctioned off.

At that moment, I felt the weight of the world on my shoulders. It was a difficult time, living on my god-sister's sofa and still grappling with the loss of our mother a few years prior. Just months prior I had what I thought was everything. My own boutique, a nice place, brand new luxury car, you name it, I had it, *(that's a story for another book)*.

I never received notification that the storage facility management changed, and I no longer had a grace period. Prior to that month, all payments were made on time and although the current payment was made, it was late- a little too late. Additional fees including a lien fee had been added. When I returned the call, it was too late. Everything was gone!

 In that storage unit were two homes worth of furniture, my diploma, all my mother's treasured belongings, clothes, expensive bags, shoes, keepsakes – our entire life.

In the face of such overwhelming loss, it's essential to acknowledge the grief we feel for the memories and material things that we've lost. These losses are a part of our lives, and they deserve to be mourned. It took my baby sister years to forgive me, and I'm not even sure if she has truly forgiven me for her things being lost in the storage.

As we grieve, let us also recognize the power we have within ourselves to overcome adversity and there is always hope for a brighter future. We must stand tall, resilient in the face of loss, and channel our pain into purpose. We are not defined by the losses we've experienced, but rather by how we rise above them. In the midst of loss do you fold and sink into a deeper place, or find the lesson in the loss. Perhaps God was making room for better, or maybe it was time for a fresh start. While we cannot change the past, we can choose to embrace the lessons our losses teach us, using them to grow stronger and more resilient. It is in these moments of despair that we can turn to our faith and seek the strength to carry on. Through prayer and reflection, we may begin to find meaning in our losses and learn from the experiences that have shaped us.

Let us use our faith and determination to transform our heartache into fuel for our journey forward. In doing so, we will not only heal ourselves, but we will also inspire those around us to find hope, strength, and the unwavering belief that better days are yet to come. By trusting in God's plan and recognizing the opportunities for growth that lie hidden in our darkest moments, we can move forward with courage and faith, creating a new chapter filled with hope, love, and the promise of better days to come.

Matthew 6:19-21 "Do not store up for yourselves treasures on earth, where moths and vermin destroy, and where thieves break in and steal. But store up for yourselves treasures in heaven, where moths and vermin do not destroy, and where thieves do not break in and steal. For where your treasure is, there your heart will be also."

Day 19: Her Prayers, My Path

Honoring A Mother's Legacy Amidst Grief and Triumph

Imagine standing on the pinnacle of your dreams, dreams that were lovingly nurtured in unison with your mother, who was your strongest pillar, your staunchest prayer warrior, and yet she isn't there to witness the glory of their fruition. Each victory, each achievement feels like a hushed echo of her prayers, a poignant reminder of her faith, and yet her physical absence creates a void in the heart of the celebration.

Life has an uncanny way of teaching us that even amidst joy, grief can carve its own space. It's in the silent moments, the smiles that are not shared, the proud glances that are missed. This heartache is peculiar, a longing for their presence, an insatiable yearning for the shared joy that once was. Remember, pain will eventually loosen its grip when you learn to release it. Releasing the pain doesn't mean erasing the memories or becoming indifferent; rather, it's a process of acceptance, acknowledging the pain, yet refusing to let it be the driving force of your life.

In these reflective moments, I hold on to the teachings my mother instilled in me, that an unwavering divine presence is always with us. Even though my earthly mother has departed, I take solace in knowing that my Heavenly Father remains, rejoicing in the blessings unfolding in my life. I choose to believe that in the grand, divine scheme, my mother too partakes in this joy. With this belief, I continue to celebrate, to live, to strive, fulfilling the dreams that we once nurtured together, cherishing her love and prayers in my heart, and honoring her memory at each milestone of my journey.

John 11:25-26 - "Jesus said to her, 'I am the resurrection and the life. The one who believes in me will live, even though they die; and whoever lives by believing in me will never die.

Day 20: I think I will be okay

Embracing Individual Healing

In the grip of grief, one can't help but question, "Will I ever be, okay?" The loss feels overwhelming, like an ocean of sorrow that threatens to pull you under. You might find yourself observing others who have faced similar loss, comparing your reactions, your timeline, your coping mechanisms. But here's a truth that bears repeating: Grief is unique, as unique as the relationship you shared with your loved one. Everyone must grieve in their own way and time.

There is no standard blueprint for grief, no one-size-fits-all solution. Just as we are all unique individuals, our experiences of grief are unique too. You may see others moving forward more quickly, or perhaps more slowly, and it's natural to compare. But your journey is your own. Embrace it. Lean into it. It's okay to be not okay, and it's okay to start feeling okay, even if it's sooner or later than others might expect.

"I think I will be okay," you say. And, dear friend, that's the glimmer of hope that shines through the dark clouds of grief. It's the recognition that while the pain of loss never fully disappears, we can learn to live with it, to carry it with us as we continue our journey. You are stronger than you think. Lean on the promises of God. Trust that you will find your way through this, in your own time, in your own way.

You will be okay.

2 Corinthians 12:9 - "My grace is sufficient for you, for my power is made perfect in weakness."

Day 21: Journey of Grace

Navigating Life's Ebbs and Flows

In the quiet moments of your nights, when the world stands still and your heart feels heavy, it's essential to acknowledge that you're not okay. Grief can be overwhelming, leaving you shattered and adrift. But here's the truth: you don't have to face this journey alone, and it's perfectly alright to embrace the complexities of your emotions.

Society often expects us to put on a brave face and move forward, but grief is a deeply personal experience that defies any timeline or expectations. Your grief is uniquely yours, and there is no one-size-fits-all approach to navigate it. Grant yourself the permission to accept the unsettledness, to sit with your pain, and to be okay with not being okay. It's through this raw vulnerability that genuine healing begins.

Amidst the anguish, remember that within you lies a wellspring of resilience that can carry you through the darkest nights. Honor your grief by giving yourself the compassion and understanding you deserve. Seek out a supportive community that can walk beside you on this path, providing solace and comfort along the way. As you navigate the waves of grief, know that there are others who understand and are ready to lend a helping hand. Embrace the truth that it's alright to not have all the answers and to allow yourself the time and space to heal.

In the depths of your grief, trust in the power of your own healing journey. Embrace the discomfort, for within it lies an opportunity to discover your inner strength and resilience. Take each step with tenderness and patience, knowing that brighter days will find you. You are a survivor, and your unique path through grief is a testament to your courage. Have faith in the transformative power that resides within you, and believe that amidst the pain, there is room for renewal, growth, and the possibility of finding joy once again.

Isaiah 41:10 - "Fear not, for I am with you; be not dismayed, for I am your God. I will strengthen you, yes, I will help you, I will uphold you with My righteous right hand."

Day 22: Finding Freedom in Self-Respect

Navigating Grief After Leaving a Toxic Workplace

Leaving a job is not always a choice made solely for career advancement or personal growth. Sometimes, it is a courageous step taken to protect our mental and emotional well-being in the face of mistreatment and discrimination. I know firsthand the anguish that accompanies such a decision—the sleepless nights, the constant anxiety, and the deep-seated wounds that linger long after walking away.

In a toxic workplace, every day can feel like an uphill battle. The mistreatment and discrimination chip away at our self-worth, leaving us questioning our abilities and doubting our value. It's a suffocating environment that drains our energy and stifles our potential. When the scales tip, and the pain outweighs the benefits, we find ourselves standing at the crossroads of self-respect and survival.

Leaving a toxic workplace is a courageous act of reclaiming our dignity and preserving our mental health. It's not an admission of defeat, but a declaration that we deserve better. As we navigate the aftermath of our departure, it's crucial to acknowledge the grief that accompanies leaving a toxic environment. Allow yourself to mourn the loss of what could have been, the dreams you had for that job, and the sense of belonging you yearned for. Give yourself permission to heal and rediscover your self-worth.

In this journey of healing, surround yourself with a support network that uplifts and validates your experiences. Seek solace in the company of loved ones, friends, and mentors who can provide a safe space for you to share your pain and process your emotions. Find strength in the stories of others who have overcome similar challenges, knowing that you are not alone in your struggles.

As you rebuild your career and navigate new opportunities, remember that your mistreatment does not define you. Your worth goes beyond the unfair treatment you endured. Believe in your capabilities, talents, and unique gifts. Embrace your resilience and tap into your inner strength as you chart a new path. Seek opportunities that align with your values and prioritize your well-being.

In the process of rebuilding, hold onto your faith and trust in God's justice. He sees the mistreatment and discrimination you faced, and He will guide you towards a brighter future. Have faith that He will bring justice and restore what was taken from you. Remember that in Him, you are fearfully and wonderfully made, deserving of respect, dignity, and love.

So, my dear friend, as you navigate the aftermath of leaving a toxic workplace, know that you are not alone. Your pain is valid, and your decision to prioritize your well-being is commendable. Embrace the healing journey, find strength in your resilience, and trust in the power of your own worth. The mistreatment you endured does not define you. You are capable of rising above, rebuilding your career, and finding fulfillment in a workplace that cherishes and respects your unique contributions.

Romans 12:19 - "Beloved, do not avenge yourselves, but rather give place to wrath; for it is written, 'Vengeance is Mine, I will repay,' says the Lord."

Day 23: A Sister's Love

The Unbreakable Bond: Grieving A Sister and Best Friend

When my best friend, who was like a little sister to me passed away in her early 20's, my heart shattered into a million pieces. She was my rock, my confidante, and my partner in life's journey. Her sudden departure left me feeling lost, and the pain of losing her was unbearable. As the mother of three beautiful children, she had so much life left to live, and the void she left behind was immense.

The last time I saw her was in the hospital, her eyes filled with a mix of fear and hope. All she wanted was a Coca-Cola, and I knew it was likely to be our final shared moment. As my fiancé now husband smuggled the drink into her room, my heart ached, and I prayed for a miracle that would never come. I remember the warmth of her hand in mine, the unspoken words of love and gratitude between us, as we prayed and said our silent goodbyes.

Her passing marked a turning point in my life; grief and sorrow consumed me. I had recently lost my aunt and mother, my heart yearned to be at her funeral, but the pain of seeing her casket and saying a final goodbye was more than I could bear. Instead, I chose to hold onto our most precious memories: the laughter-filled summer days, cooking and eating good, trips to the flea market (if you are from Ft. Lauderdale, you know the spot) to take pictures, the many hairstyles she practiced on me, our late-night heart-to-hearts, and the unbreakable bond we had forged. The pain of losing her still lingers, yet I know that she would want me to find strength and courage in the face of adversity.

In the depths of my grief, I have discovered that our love transcends the boundaries of life and death. And so, as I continue to heal, I choose to honor her memory by living a life filled with love, compassion, and purpose, knowing that her spirit will forever be by my side.

Matthew 11:28 - "Come to Me, all you who labor and are heavy laden, and I will give you rest."

Day 24: I can't breathe

Breathing Through Unthinkable Loss, Healing from Revengeful Hurt

The news crashed into my life like a storm, leaving behind unimaginable pain. The loss of a loved one to senseless violence thrust me into suffocating grief, fueled by revengeful hurt. In my shattered heart, I cried out to God, seeking hope, healing, and the strength to forgive. It was in those desperate moments that I discovered His presence as my refuge, offering guidance towards healing.

As I embarked on the journey of healing, I realized that revengeful hurt can be a formidable obstacle to overcome. Recognizing this, I discovered several essential steps to navigate this painful path. I chose to confront my emotions honestly, acknowledging the depth of my hurt and anger. Through prayer and seeking support from trusted friends or counselors, I found a safe space to express and process these intense feelings. The road to healing involved cultivating a heart of forgiveness. While forgiveness may seem daunting, I learned that it is a choice—an intentional decision to release the desire for revenge and entrust justice to a higher power. By surrendering my need for retribution, I opened myself to the transformative power of forgiveness, experiencing the freedom that comes from letting go of the heavy burden of revengeful hurt.

In God's embrace, we find the strength to take these steps and breathe deeply, allowing His healing presence to restore our wounded hearts.

Proverbs 20:22 - "Do not say, 'I will recompense evil'; wait for the Lord, and He will save you."

Day 25: The Silence After the Farewells

Embracing Solitude as A Path to Healing

Now that everyone has gone home, I find myself in the company of silence. The comforting hum of friends and family has faded, leaving me alone with my thoughts and the weight of my grief. It feels as if I am adrift at sea, navigating through the tumultuous waves of heartache. Yet, in this solitude, I discover a glimmer of strength—a quiet resilience that whispers, "You can endure this."

I remind myself that it's okay to feel the pain, to sit with it, and acknowledge its presence. This journey of grief is unique, and it unfolds in our own time and in our own way. In these moments of solitude, I find solace in leaning on God, seeking comfort in His word and His promises. As the psalmist declares in Psalm 34:18, "The Lord is close to the brokenhearted and saves those who are crushed in spirit." Even in the stillness, I am not alone.

So, as I sit here in the silence, I encourage myself—and you—to embrace these moments of solitude. Let them become spaces of reflection, healing, and growth. It's okay to let the tears flow, for each tear is a testament to the depth of our love, a symbol of our resilience, and a step towards healing. In this quiet place, we can draw closer to God, finding strength and comfort in His presence. Though the road ahead may be long, we can endure, for even in the silence, we are accompanied by a love that never fades.

In the silence that follows the farewells, we discover a profound opportunity for healing and growth. Embrace these moments of solitude, for they are not empty, but filled with the presence of God. In the depths of your grief, know that you are not alone. Lean on Him, seek solace in His promises, and allow the tears to flow. Each moment of silence is a chance to reflect, heal, and grow stronger. With every step, you move closer to the light that awaits you on the other side. Embrace the silence, for it is in this stillness that you will find the strength to rise and embrace a new day.

Psalm 147:3 - "He heals the brokenhearted and binds up their wounds."

Day 26: From Prognosis to Deliverance

Faith, Resilience, And Miraculous Healing

I want to share with you a heartfelt and remarkable story that unfolded before my eyes. It is a story of my beloved god sister J, whom I affectionately call "babes." Her journey has been one of unimaginable challenges and incredible miracles—a testament to the boundless grace of God and the power of faith.

Months after receiving the devastating news that she had only three months to live, J finally found the courage to share her secret with me. The weight of her diagnosis had been silently crushing her spirit, and it took immense strength to open up about the struggle she had been enduring. It was a moment that shook me to the core, realizing that she had carried this burden in solitude for so long.

But even in the face of such overwhelming despair, she held on to a glimmer of hope. Through a series of blood transfusions, over a month in the hospital and the miraculous gift of double organ donations after only days on the donor list, she defied all odds and emerged from the brink of death. It was a moment of divine intervention, a reminder that even in the darkest of times, miracles can still happen.

Although J survived, her journey was far from over. The experience forever changed her, reshaping her perspective on life and the purpose she was meant to fulfill. It was a bittersweet realization that while she was given a second chance, she would never be the same person she was before. Life has a way of thrusting us into situations that alter us at the core, leaving indelible marks on our souls. But within these transformations lie the seeds of growth, resilience, and a deeper appreciation for the fleeting beauty of life.

As we navigate the aftermath of life-altering experiences, we are reminded that our purpose on this earth is far greater than we can comprehend. J's miraculous survival was not a coincidence; it was a testament to the remarkable journey she was meant to embark upon. Though she may never be the same person, she carries within her a profound sense of purpose and a determination to make every moment count. Life changes us, molds us, and presents us with opportunities to rise above our circumstances. It is in embracing these transformations that we can uncover our true potential and inspire those around us.

From the depths of despair to the miraculous transformation of life, J's journey reminds us of the power of faith and the resilience of the human spirit. We each carry the weight of our own life changes, and although we may never be the same, we can embrace the purpose that emerges from our experiences. Our stories, marked by trials and triumphs, shape us into vessels of inspiration and hope. Let us recognize the magnitude of our purpose and the impact we can have on others, for even in the midst of life's storms, miracles are waiting to unfold. Embrace your transformations and step into the greatness that lies within you. I can't wait for J to share her story with the world, stay tuned!

Deuteronomy 31:6 - "Be strong and courageous. Do not be afraid or terrified because of them, for the Lord your God goes with you; he will never leave you nor forsake you."

Day 27: Unfinished Sentences

Grieving The Words Left Unsaid

We often assume we'll have all the time in the world to say the things we need to, the things we want to. But when that time abruptly ends, we are left with a pocket full of words, unsaid, unfinished, lingering in the silence. Maybe it was an apology you wanted to extend, a thank you, an I love you. Or perhaps a story you meant to share, a dream, a hope, a fear. The weight of these unsaid words can be a heavy burden to bear, a constant reminder of the finality of loss.

The silence can be deafening, the unsaid words echoing in the empty spaces. And it's easy to get lost in the 'what ifs,' in the regret of not having said more, done more.

As you navigate through the rough waves of grief, hold onto the faith that God knows your heart, He understands the depth of your love and your loss. The love you have, the words you couldn't say, He knows them all. In time, may you find comfort in the unsaid, knowing that love was communicated in ways beyond words. And in time, may the burden of the unsaid become lighter, replaced by the cherished memories and the eternal love you hold.

Psalms 56:8 tells us, "You keep track of all my sorrows. You have collected all my tears in your bottle. You have recorded each one in your book."

Day 28: *Why didn't I just call?*

"The Weight of Regret and the Power of Healing"

That morning remains etched in my memory with painful clarity. I remember speaking to my aunt, our voices carrying across the phone lines, oblivious to the fate that awaited her. She was on her way to visit a friend, and we eagerly anticipated her return for a wedding rehearsal. But the hours passed, and she never showed up. Something tugged at my heart, a nagging feeling to call her earlier, but I dismissed it. Later that day we all tried to reach her bit no answer. Instead, I got dressed and went out to dinner, unaware of the tragedy unfolding.

Upon my return, the ringing of the phone shattered the evening's tranquility. My mom's anguished voice pierced through the line, screaming and crying. It was my best friend who was at my mom's house, whose presence is now but a memory, delivering the crushing news. Something had happened to my aunt. Panic seized me as I raced to her house, my cousin standing in the doorway, his eyes streaming tears. The police were there, holding her driver's license, confirming the tragedy. Grief crashed over us like a relentless wave, stealing the air from our lungs. Later, we would come to learn that my aunt had died in a car accident, the belief being that she had fallen asleep at the wheel. Witnesses spoke of a swerving car, flipping into the water. Attempts were made to save her, but the water was unforgiving. Broken glass and retrieved clothing would be the haunting remnants of the crash. They found her lifeless body in the backseat. I remember questioning myself, if I had made the call, would the ring have jolted her awake?

The weight of grief settled upon our shoulders, an immeasurable pain that no family should bear. My cousins were left shattered, hearts heavy with loss. It felt as though the world had come crashing down, engulfing us in a darkness that seemed insurmountable. We realized that healing would be a gradual journey, and that each of us would grieve in our own way and time. Most of us are still struggling with grief, and that's okay. Though the scars of loss remain, we have learned to carry our loved ones' memories in our hearts, allowing their light to guide us toward healing and eventual restoration.

Healing will come, gradually and with time, as we carry our loved ones' memories with us, allowing their light to guide us toward restoration. May we find comfort in knowing that they live on within us, and may their legacy inspire us to embrace life fully, *(my Aunt C lived life!)* cherishing each precious moment we are given.

Proverbs 3:5-6 - "Trust in the Lord with all your heart and lean not on your own understanding; in all your ways submit to him, and he will make your paths straight."

Day 29: Will I Make It?

Embracing The Power Within

In the depths of grief, there are moments when the road ahead feels impassable. The weight of loss sits heavy on our hearts, and we find ourselves asking, "Will I make it?" It's a question whispered in vulnerability, echoing through the chambers of our soul. In these moments, the future seems uncertain, devoid of hope and color. But hold on, for there is a truth that anchors us in the midst of the storm.

The truth is you will make it. This is not a hollow assurance, but a declaration of faith grounded in the promises of God. In Jeremiah 29:11, we are reminded of His plans for us - plans to prosper, to give hope, and to lead us into a future filled with purpose. God's promise is not a quick fix that erases our pain; it is a steady beacon of hope that guides us through the darkest nights.

So, cling to this promise with unwavering faith. Allow it to infuse you with strength and courage. Though the journey may be long, and obstacles may arise, remember that you are stronger than you know, braver than you feel, and deeply loved by your Heavenly Father. Step by step, moment by moment, with God by your side, you will make it. Embrace the resilience within you, draw from the wellspring of His grace, and trust that He will carry you through to a place of healing, restoration, and renewed purpose.

In the face of grief's overwhelming challenges, remember that you are not alone. God, who holds the universe in His hands, also holds your heart. You are resilient, capable of enduring and rising above the pain. Embrace His promises, let them be the foundation upon which you rebuild. With each step forward, you are forging a path of strength, hope, and resilience. Your story isn't over, and the best is yet to come. Keep pressing on, for you will make it.

Jeremiah 29:11 - "For I know the thoughts that I think toward you, says the LORD, thoughts of peace and not of evil, to give you a future and a hope."

Day 30: Why are you pushing me away?

Supporting a Grieving loved One with Grace

In the tumultuous journey of grief, there are moments when it feels like you're standing on opposite sides of a vast chasm, desperately trying to bridge the gap between you and your grieving spouse or loved one. You offer your support, your love, your presence, only to be met with resistance and distance. It's an agonizing experience, feeling shut out and misunderstood, unsure of how to navigate this uncharted territory. But in these moments of frustration and longing, remember that grief is as unique as a fingerprint, and everyone processes it in their own way and time.

It's essential to recognize that your loved one's withdrawal isn't a personal rejection, but a manifestation of their own pain and confusion. Grief is an intricate dance of emotions, and sometimes it's easier to push away those closest to us rather than confront the depths of our sorrow. While it may be challenging, try to approach their grieving journey with empathy and understanding. Offer them a safe space to express their emotions without judgment and be patient as they navigate the labyrinth of grief.

Although it may feel like you're on separate paths, there is hope. By extending unwavering support and patience, you create a foundation for healing and connection. Remember, love has the power to bridge even the widest chasms. In due time, your love may find solace in your presence and lean on you for comfort. Together, you can emerge from the shadows of grief, stronger and more united than ever before. So, hold on to hope, my friend, for even during this turbulent journey, love can transcend the barriers of grief and lead you both to a place of healing and renewed connection.

Proverbs 17:17 - "A friend loves at all times, and a brother is born for adversity."

Day 31: Overcoming the Shadows

Embracing The Not-So-Good Days

Let's be real, there are days when the sun doesn't seem to shine as brightly, when the weight of the world feels unbearable, and when all you want to do is pull the covers over your head and retreat from the world. I've been there - we've all been there. Days when grief feels like a bitter, relentless storm that shows no sign of passing. Days when you're left questioning, "Why me?" and "How much more can I take?". These are the not-so-good days, the days when despair threatens to consume you.

Remember this, the not-so-good days are not an indication of weakness, nor are they a reflection of your faith. They are simply part of the human experience, part of the journey of healing and growth. It's okay to feel the pain, to acknowledge the hurt, and to give yourself the permission to grieve. These moments of vulnerability are not your downfall, but rather an opportunity for deeper self-understanding and compassion.

The key lies not in avoiding these days but in facing them head-on, armed with faith, resilience, and the knowledge that this too shall pass. You're stronger than your worst day, braver than your deepest fears, and more resilient than your greatest challenges. Remember, every storm runs out of rain, and every night gives way to a new dawn. As you navigate the rough seas of grief, may you find comfort in knowing that even the most turbulent storms serve a purpose - they clear the path, making way for new growth, new beginnings, and a newfound strength that you never knew you possessed.

Embrace the not-so-good days, for they are a testament to your human capacity to feel, to love, and to endure. And when you find yourself during the storm, remember that the sun still shines above the clouds. You are not alone. You are seen. You are loved. And most importantly, you are capable of weathering this storm.

Peter 5:10 - "But may the God of all grace, who called us to His eternal glory by Christ Jesus, after you have suffered a while, perfect, establish, strengthen, and settle you."

Day 32: Questions

Trusting God's Sovereignty in The Midst of Grief

In the depths of grief, it's natural for questions to flood our minds. We wrestle with the why, the how, and the what-ifs. It can feel like we're standing on shaky ground, longing for answers that seem elusive. Yet, in the midst of our questioning, we must remember that our human understanding is limited. As Isaiah 55:8 reminds us, God's thoughts are not our thoughts, and His ways are not our ways. It's a humbling realization that invites us to trust in His wisdom and surrender our need for immediate answers.

When faced with profound loss, we may struggle to find meaning in the midst of pain. But even in the darkest moments, we can find solace in the knowledge that God's plan is still at work. He can take the broken pieces of our lives and create something beautiful. Our pain becomes a catalyst for growth, compassion, and strength. Though we may not understand the reasons behind our suffering, we can trust in God's unfailing love and His promise to never abandon us. He walks with us through the storm, guiding us with a wisdom that surpasses our understanding.

So, as the questions continue to swirl and uncertainty persists, let us anchor our hearts in trust. Trust that God sees the bigger picture, even when we cannot. Trust that He is working all things together for our good, even in the face of devastating loss. And trust that, in His perfect timing, He will bring healing and restoration. Embrace the journey of grief, knowing that it is unique and personal to you. Seek comfort in His presence, find solace in His Word, and allow His wisdom to guide you through the depths of your sorrow.

"In the midst of grief's relentless questions, let us find solace in trusting God's infinite wisdom. Though we may not understand His ways, He holds the power to transform our pain into purpose. Embrace the journey of grief, knowing that it is a path uniquely crafted for you. As you surrender your questions to God, may you discover a peace that surpasses all understanding. Take comfort in His presence, lean on His promises, and allow His love to carry you through the darkest nights. In Him, there is hope, healing, and a future that shines brighter than any sorrow."

Psalm 46:10 - "Be still, and know that I am God; I will be exalted among the nations, I will be exalted in the earth"

Day 33: When Time Runs Short

Contemplating Their Final Days

The realization that our time on this earth is limited is a sobering thought that shakes us to the core. As I reflect on those who received the devastating news that they had only days to live, I can't help but wonder what thoughts raced through their minds in those final moments. Did they ponder the dreams left unfulfilled, the moments they wished they could have shared with loved ones? Were there regrets that weighed heavily on their hearts, or did they find solace in the beauty of the life they had lived? The truth is, we may never fully grasp the depth of their thoughts and emotions in those final days. But it serves as a poignant reminder that life is fragile, and each moment is a precious gift to be cherished.

In the face of such profound brevity, I am confronted with the uniqueness of grief and the individuality of each person's journey. We cannot fully comprehend the range of emotions and reflections that consumed those who faced their final days. Grief, much like life, is a deeply personal experience that defies simple explanations or cliché statements. It is a tapestry woven with the complexities of human emotion, the interplay of joy and sorrow, love and loss. It is in recognizing this individuality that we can approach grief with compassion and understanding, allowing each person the freedom to process their emotions in their own way and time.

Contemplating the thoughts of those who faced their imminent passing, I am reminded of the importance of living fully and embracing each moment. We are gifted with this precious life, and it is up to us to make the most of the time we have. Let us not wait until faced with our own mortality to reflect on what truly matters. Instead, let us seize each day as an opportunity to love, to forgive, and to pursue our passions. In the face of the uncertainty of life, we can find solace in the knowledge that our time on this earth is not determined by the quantity, but rather the quality of our experiences. May we live with purpose, compassion, and a deep appreciation for the brevity and beauty of life.

Each person's journey through grief is as unique as the thoughts that raced through their minds during those final moments. Let us approach grief with compassion, recognizing that everyone processes their emotions in their own way and time. In the face of mortality, let us live fully, embracing each day as a gift. May we seize every opportunity to love, forgive, and pursue our passions, for in doing so, we honor the brevity and beauty of this precious life we've been given.

James 4:14 - "whereas you do not know what will happen tomorrow. For what is your life? It is even a vapor that appears for a little time and then vanishes away."

Day 34: When Grief Knocks on the Family's Door

Navigating Family Dynamics and Finding Unity in Grief

Grief is a messy journey that can turn our family dynamics upside down when a loved one passes away. It's no secret that family members can sometimes act out, argue, or even bring chaos into the mix during our most vulnerable moments. It can be bewildering and frustrating, but it's important to remember that grief affects everyone differently. Each person carries their own baggage, unresolved issues, and unique ways of coping. By understanding and respecting these differences, we can navigate the challenges and find unity amidst the chaos.

When we hope that the pain of loss will bring our family closer, it can be disheartening to witness arguments, power struggles, and even severed ties. However, it's essential to recognize that grief is overwhelming, often bringing out the best and worst in people. Our family members may be acting out of their own pain, fear, or frustration. Instead of judging or resenting them, let's choose compassion and understanding. By doing so, we create an atmosphere of healing, providing space for reconciliation and unity.

In the face of family turmoil during times of loss, we have an opportunity to break free from cycles of pain and dysfunction. Choosing forgiveness over resentment, compassion over judgment, and love over discord can pave the way for healing and create a legacy for generations to come. While it's not an easy path to walk, it's one that honors the memory of our departed loved ones and transforms our family dynamics. Let's remember that grief is personal, and everyone's journey is unique. Together, we can navigate the storms, support one another, and rise above the chaos, demonstrating the transformative power of love and unity in the face of grief.

Amidst the chaos of family dynamics in grief, we have a choice: to let the turmoil tear us apart or to rise above it, finding unity, healing, and even humor along the way. By extending compassion and understanding, we break free from cycles of pain and dysfunction, creating a brighter, more united future. So, let's embrace the messy, navigate the challenges, and remember that laughter can be a powerful balm for the soul, even in the most difficult of times.

1 Peter 4:8-9 - "And above all things have fervent love for one another, for 'love will cover a multitude of sins.' Be hospitable to one another without grumbling."

Day 35: The Complex Tides and Delicate Dance of Grief

Acknowledging a Past Partner's Impact While Cherishing a Current love

When the news arrives that a cherished mentor, who once held a more intimate place in one's life, has passed away, it can feel like the world has suddenly shifted on its axis. This mentor is not merely a guiding figure; they are also a friend, and the relationship, though no longer romantic, carries a significant imprint on one's life.

The challenges of balancing the grief of a loss and maintaining the stability of one's current relationship can be demanding. Especially when the bond formed with the mentor has contributed deeply to personal and professional growth. The mentor's impact remains a potent force, their teachings and guidance resonating in the pursuit of one's dreams.

There might be concern about how to handle the grief, fearing judgment from others. To grieve too openly may seem inappropriate given the current relationship status, while not acknowledging the loss may give the impression of indifference.

However, it's essential to realize that mourning is a deeply individual process, and there's no one right way to navigate it. The most crucial aspect is to allow oneself to grieve and to honor the departed mentor's memory.

The sense of loss might be profound, but comfort can be found in the lessons learned from the mentor. Despite their physical absence, their spirit continues to influence those whose lives they've touched, providing a source of solace.

As one continues to mature and progress, the wisdom and guidance received from the mentor become an enduring part of one's personal and professional identity. It serves as a constant reminder that human connections can be so powerful and impactful that they transcend the boundaries of life and death, becoming an integral part of one's own journey, even after the physical presence has ceased.

And so, life continues. The mentor's legacy lives on within, inspiring resilience and dedication. Amid the grief and memories, there lies an opportunity to transform personal sorrow into strength, to honor the mentor's teachings by living them out in daily life, to further nurture current relationships, and to build upon the wisdom gained. For the impact of such a profound connection never truly fades—it only fuels the ongoing journey towards growth and fulfillment.

Matthew 5:4 - "Blessed are those who mourn, for they shall be comforted."

Day 36: From Grief to Growth

Embracing The Journey of Self-Transformation After Loss

Grief is a deeply intimate journey that carves its way into the very core of our being. It shatters our world, leaving us lost amidst the fragments of our shattered hearts. Yet, within the depths of this pain lies the untold story of our own transformation. It is a path that is uniquely ours, as we navigate the twists and turns of grief's labyrinth. There is no prescribed timeline for healing, no one-size-fits-all approach. We must honor our own rhythm, granting ourselves the grace and space to navigate this uncharted territory.

As we traverse the unpredictable terrain of grief, we often find ourselves grappling with profound questions and searching for meaning amidst the ache. We may question the purpose of our suffering, wondering how such heartbreak could possibly lead to growth. Yet, it is in these moments of deep introspection that we begin to unearth the hidden seeds of strength within us. Through vulnerability and self-reflection, we have the chance to discover the invaluable lessons and insights that lie dormant beneath the surface. By embracing the full spectrum of our emotions, from the darkest shadows to the glimmers of hope, we embark on a transformative journey of self-discovery.

Within the crucible of grief, we possess the power to cultivate resilience, wisdom, and compassion. It is a journey that demands unwavering courage and an unwavering commitment to our own healing. As we walk this path, we find solace in the stories of others who have weathered their own storms and emerged with a renewed sense of purpose. We draw strength from their experiences, knowing that we are not alone in our struggles. It is through the integration of our grief that we begin to embrace a new version of ourselves, one forged in the fires of loss but infused with newfound depth and understanding. In the sacred space of our journey, we rise from the ashes, revealing our own strength and inspiring others to embrace their unique path of self-transformation.

As we navigate the uncharted territory of grief, may we trust in our own wisdom and intuition. We possess the power to emerge from the depths, carrying the torch of our transformation and illuminating the way for others to find their own strength and embrace their unique path of self-transformation. Let us become living embodiments of hope, reminding the world that even in the face of unimaginable loss, we have the power to rise and shine.

Romans 8:18 - "I consider that our present sufferings are not worth comparing with the glory that will be revealed in us."

Day 37: Healing Hearts

Honoring Love While Embracing New Life, Fatherhood, And Rediscovering Love

In the panorama of life, joy and sorrow often walk hand in hand. Picture this, a man, bathed in the dichotomy of life's deepest emotions. He cradles new life in his arms, a beacon of joy and hope, but also the embodiment of an unforgettable loss. His partner, his love, his confidante has just given her life in the act of creating another. The echo of her laughter still lingers in their home, a poignant memory etched in every corner. Suddenly, he finds himself in a delicate dance between cherishing a new life and mourning a profound loss, preserving her legacy not just for himself, but for their child as well.

Grief, as we all know, isn't a straight path. It's a winding road with peaks of acceptance and valleys of sorrow. In the quiet moments, broken only by the soft coos and cries of their newborn, he grapples with a myriad of emotions. But as the days turn into weeks and months, he begins to see that while he holds the mantle of their past, he is also the beacon for their child's future. He realizes that, in honoring her memory, he also honors life, resilience, and the indomitable human spirit - the very qualities she embodied.

Navigating the possibility of new love while preserving the memory of a departed one isn't about replacement; it's about growth. It's understanding that love, in its purest form, isn't finite or constrained, but expansive and all-embracing. As he looks into their child's eyes, he sees her spirit, a testament to a love that transcends physical boundaries. Through the ebb and flow of grief, raising their child, and embracing the potential for new love, he discovers that moving forward isn't about forgetting the past, but about carrying it forward with grace, love, and resilience. This journey becomes a powerful testament to life's enduring capacity for love and transformation, reminding us all that even in the face of loss and pain, hope prevails, and love endures.

Psalm 46:1-2 "God is our refuge and strength, an ever-present help in trouble. Therefore, we will not fear, though the earth gives way, and the mountains fall into the heart of the sea."

Day 38: God, please help me get up!

Rising from The Paralyzing Grip of Grief

In the depths of grief, when the weight of loss threatens to suffocate us, even the simplest acts of daily living feel insurmountable. It's as if the world has paused, while our hearts remain stuck in a state of despair. We question how we will ever find the strength to rise again, to eat, to shower, to move forward.

When we find ourselves immobilized by sorrow, it's crucial to extend compassion and grace to ourselves. Grief is not a linear process with a fixed timeline. It's a maze of emotions, and we each have our own path to navigate. It's okay to take small steps, to lean on others for support, and to seek professional help if needed. Healing takes time, and every step, no matter how small, is a victory.

While the pain of grief is undeniable, there is hope even in the depths of despair. The small victories, like getting out of bed or nourishing our bodies, become beacons of hope, reminders that we are capable of resilience and growth. So, even in the darkest moments, hold on to the flicker of light, for it is a sign that healing is possible, and brighter days will come.

Isaiah 40:31 - "But they who wait for the Lord shall renew their strength; they shall mount up with wings like eagles; they shall run and not be weary; they shall walk and not faint".

Day 39: Embracing the Uniqueness of Grief

Your Journey, Your Pace

Dear friend, let us sit together in this space, feeling the echoes of lost love. Your grief is uniquely yours, and it's okay to lean into it, to not quite understand it. It doesn't come with a manual, no standard step-by-step guide to follow, for grief is not a problem to be solved, but a journey to be walked.

In the hours when silence is deafening and loneliness swells like an ocean wave, remember, it's okay to grieve in your way, at your pace. Your grief is not a race, there are no milestones you must meet. It's a personal journey, an intimate conversation between you and the pain you carry. You don't need to fit into the expectations of others or the world.

With each breath, I invite you to whisper into your pain, saying, "I see you. I hear you. I will walk with you." Just as a seed must crack and break to sprout into a tree, your grief can foster growth and healing in its own time. Remember, dear friend, you have the strength to weather this storm. You are a lighthouse amidst these troubled waters, stronger and braver than you think.

Lamentations 3:22-23: "Because of the LORD's great love we are not consumed, for his compassions never fail. They are new every morning; great is your faithfulness."

Day 40: Grief's Path to Recovery

Surrendering the Past, Embracing the Present: Finding Healing and Renewal After Addiction

In the depths of addiction's grip, many have found themselves lost in a world of chaos and despair. The allure of substances can ensnare even the most vibrant souls, leaving behind a trail of shattered dreams and fractured relationships. It is a battle that not only affects the individual, but also their loved ones who must witness their transformation. Grief becomes a constant companion, as we mourn the person our loved one once was and grapple with the pain they have caused. It is a journey of deep sorrow and profound resilience, one that requires us to navigate the complexities of grief while finding the strength to embrace a new chapter.

Within the turmoil of addiction and its ripple effects, there is hope. We must learn to grieve not only for the person our loved one once was, but also for the life we envisioned for them. We let go of our expectations and accept the reality of the present. It is a painful process, but within this journey, we discover the power of unconditional love and unwavering support. As we stand by their side, offering empathy and understanding, we become pillars of strength for their recovery.

Through this arduous path, both the individual battling addiction and their loved ones experience their own forms of grief. But in the midst of this pain, there is a glimmer of light. Recovery is possible. With professional help, support networks, and a commitment to healing, lives can be transformed. It is a testament to the resilience of the human spirit and the capacity for growth and redemption. So, to those who find themselves in the midst of this battle, hold onto hope. Seek solace in the knowledge that you are not alone, and that there are brighter days ahead. Embrace the journey, embrace the process of healing, and know that you have the power to rebuild a life filled with love, joy, and purpose.

2 Corinthians 5:17 - "Therefore, if anyone is in Christ, the new creation has come: The old has gone, the new is here!"

Day 41: Beyond 'I'm Sorry

Journeying Through Guilt and Grief to Self-Forgiveness

If your heart is feeling the aching emptiness of a loved one's absence, you might also be wrestling with the guilt of an unexpressed apology. The 'I'm sorry' that you wish you had said might be echoing in your mind, amplifying the sound of your loss. In this solitary quiet, I offer you an understanding hand. I may not know the exact contours of your grief, but I do understand the rough texture of guilt and the longing for words unsaid.

Yet, even in this weighty silence, your apology was spoken in countless ways. Each act of kindness was a syllable, each shared laughter a sentence, each tender glance a paragraph. Your apology lived in the daily dance of love you both shared. Remember, language extends beyond the realm of words. It reaches into the silence, into the actions, into the everyday. The remorse now occupying your heart merely testifies to the immense depth of your love. This guilt, heavy as it may seem, is also the scale that measures your capacity to love, to care, and to regret.

Now, it is time to journey from regret towards healing. Allow this guilt to be your compass, guiding you towards empathy, understanding, and self-forgiveness. Yes, forgiveness. Forgiving yourself may seem like a mountainous task, but each step forward, no matter how small, is a step towards the summit. Let the love you have for your departed loved one illuminate your path. It is not the shadow that falls behind you but the light that leads ahead. As you traverse this unique journey of grief, find strength in the knowledge that you are more than the 'sorry' left unsaid. You are the culmination of the love shared, the memories created, and the life lived with your loved one. With each sunrise, may you find a renewed sense of hope, a nudge to forgive yourself, and a reminder of the boundless love that remains. And in the quiet of the sunset, may you find peace, knowing that you've done enough, loved enough, and it's okay to let go of the guilt and embrace the healing.

Psalm 103:12 - "As far as the east is from the west, so far has he removed our transgressions from us."

Day 42: Navigating the Waves of Grief

Anchoring Through the Storms of Heartache

Let us acknowledge that grief comes in waves. Some days you may feel steady, while others may feel like you're drowning in a sea of despair. This fluctuation is part of the journey, a testament to the love you've lost, but also a testament to the love that still resides within you.

Loss brings an uninvited change. A chair left empty, a laugh missing from the chorus, a pair of shoes that will never be worn again. And yet, life insists on continuing around us. Remember, it's okay to pause, to sit in your grief, to acknowledge the empty spaces.

As the waves of grief ebb and flow, know that each wave you weather strengthens you, even if it doesn't feel like it. Each wave is a testament to your resilience, your capacity for love, and your ability to endure. Know that with each wave, you are not alone.

Psalm 55:22 "Cast your cares on the LORD and he will sustain you; he will never let the righteous be shaken.

Day 43: The Silent Language of Grief

Understanding The Unspoken Words of Loss

There's a language to grief that words often fail to capture. It's in the tears that fall when you stumble upon their favorite book, the sighs that escape when you catch a scent they wore, the ache that fills your chest on quiet evenings. Your grief speaks, and it's okay to listen.

In this dialogue with your grief, you may find a well of resilience and wisdom. By sitting in the silence, you allow yourself to fully feel the gravity of your loss. And in this, there's a strange kind of beauty—an unfiltered acknowledgement of the depth of your love and the breadth of your loss.

Remember, it's okay to sit with your grief, to hear its silent language, to let it move through you in waves. Your grief is not a sign of weakness but a testament to your love. Listen to it, honor it, and remember that you are not alone in this journey.

John 14:27 -"Peace I leave with you; my peace I give you. I do not give to you as the world gives. Do not let your hearts be troubled and do not be afraid."

Day 44: The Landscape of Grief

A Journey Through the Terrain of Loss

Think of your grief as a landscape—a vast, expansive terrain that stretches as far as the eye can see. Some days, it might resemble a desolate desert, barren and empty. Other days, it might be a stormy sea, turbulent and unrelenting. Each day brings a different scenery, a different facet of your grief.

Navigating this landscape isn't easy. The path may be filled with pitfalls and stumbling blocks. Yet, remember, every landscape, no matter how bleak, has the potential for change. Rain can turn a desert into a blossoming oasis, and the stormy sea can become calm under the touch of the morning sun.

As you journey through your landscape of grief, know that every step you take, every challenge you overcome, is a testament to your resilience, your courage, and your capacity for love. Your journey is uniquely yours, marked by the footprints you leave behind. And remember, dear friend, no matter how vast or challenging the landscape appears, you never walk alone.

 Matthew 11:28- "Come to me, all you who are weary and burdened, and I will give you rest."

Day 45: Went Missing!

Embracing Solitude

As I sat by the bay, contemplating the words I would pour into this devotional book, a stranger approached me. His eyes held a profound sadness, yet a glimmer of hope shone through as he struck up a conversation. He asked if I wanted him to take a picture of me, but I politely declined. Undeterred, he continued to share his story, revealing that he had recently moved back to the area after losing his wife to cancer. He explained that the ocean had always been a source of solace for them both, and he was drawn to its healing power during his time of grief.

As we spoke, he revealed that in his darkest moments, he had "gone missing" - disconnecting from friends, family, and the world around him. The raw honesty of his words resonated deeply within me, reminding me of the reason I was writing this book on grief. I felt a divine nudge that urged me to share a few words of comfort and encouragement with him. We parted ways, each grateful for the unexpected connection and the reassurance that our paths were divinely guided.

We all face moments when we yearn for solitude, when the weight of our grief becomes too much to bear. It's important to acknowledge these feelings and give ourselves permission to withdraw from the world, if only for a little while. It's during these times that we can reflect on our emotions, process our pain, and start to rebuild ourselves piece by piece.

We must remember, though, that solitude is not meant to be permanent; it's only a temporary respite in our journey of healing.

In the quiet moments of solitude, we can find the strength to face our grief and begin to heal. As we emerge from this period of withdrawal, we can use our newfound understanding to better support others who may be experiencing similar pain. By sharing our stories and lending a listening ear to those in need, we create a compassionate community where healing and hope can flourish.

While the urge to "go missing" may be strong, remember that it's only a steppingstone in our path to healing, and that the love and support of those around us will help guide us back to a place of hope and resilience.

Romans 8:28 - "And we know that in all things God works for the good of those who love him, who have been called according to his purpose."

Conclusion

As we conclude our journey together through these pages, I implore you to always be gentle with yourself. Take the time to nourish your mind, body, and spirit, and never hesitate to lean on the support of your loved ones. Above all, grant yourself the permission to grieve in your own way, on your own terms, and at a pace that feels right to you.

Allow the strength and resilience of your community to uplift and fortify you. Most importantly, give yourself the freedom to express your grief authentically, without the constraints of external timelines or judgments.

Remember, there is no standardized formula or definitive roadmap for navigating grief. Each path is unique, as individual as the person walking it. And while the journey may at times feel solitary, you are part of an unspoken brotherhood and sisterhood, bound together by the shared experience of loss.

I want to express my deepest gratitude for joining me on this expedition, for delving into grief and exploring its intricate facets. It is my sincere hope that the shared experiences and insights within these pages have provided you with solace and ignited a flame of inspiration within your soul.

May you find tranquility, embrace optimism, and discover profound healing as you carve your own path through your personal journey of grief.

With boundless love and unwavering compassion,
Victoria Celeste

About The Author:

Victoria Celeste

A resilient and multi-talented Florida native and army veteran has built a diverse, inspiring and impactful career as a Certified Life Coach, Published Author, Celebrity Fashion Stylist, CEO and founder of Proper Men's Skincare and 19th and Bell Lifestyle Consulting. Despite facing personal challenges and significant losses, she persevered and established herself in entertainment industry. Victoria founded 19th and Bell Lifestyle Consulting to inspire and empower others, helping them triumph over their obstacles. Her educational background includes a Business Management degree from Ohio Christian University, a master's certification in Life and Business Coaching from Grand Canyon University and an Executive DEI certification from Cornell University. Beyond her professional accomplishments, Victoria is passionate about advocating for domestic violence and ending world hunger. In her leisure time, she embraces her faith, cherishes moments with family, and enjoys the ocean.

Contact:

www.19thandbell.com
empower@19thandbell.com
IG: @veeceleste
FB:@victoriaceleste

www.ingramcontent.com/pod-product-compliance
Lightning Source LLC
Chambersburg PA
CBHW072209090426
42740CB00012B/2451